our new baby

*For Hugo, Charlie and Dominic, without whom we would have had
to pay models to do this book. Thank you for choosing us.*

*We are indebted to the Mercy Family Birth Centre for three magnificent
and empowering births. We feel deep gratitude towards the creative and
supportive midwives who are full of wisdom and faith in the
miraculous process of pregnancy, labour and birth.*

Thomas C. Lothian Pty Ltd
132 Albert Road, South Melbourne, Victoria 3205
www.lothian.com.au

Text copyright © Catherine Deveny 2004
Photographs copyright © Mario Borg 2004

The authors may be contacted on deveny@ozemail.com.au

First published 2004

National Library of Australia
Cataloguing-in-Publication data

Deveny, Catherine.
  Our new baby.

  For children.
  ISBN 0 7344 0611 8.

  1. Pregnancy - Juvenile literature. 2. Childbirth -
  Juvenile literature. 3. Family - Juvenile literature. I.
  Borg, Mario. II. Title.

612.63

Designed by Michelle Mackintosh
Prepress by Digital Imaging Group, Port Melbourne
Printed in China by SNP Leefung

our new baby

Written by Catherine Deveny Photographs by Mario Borg

Lothian BOOKS

My name is Dominic and
I am almost five years old.

I like planes, swimming and
playing with my friends.

But most of all I *love* chocolate.

Up top is my mum Catherine and my dad Mario, and my dad with my brother Hugo, who is one year old. Underneath is Hugo again, then Hugo, Dad and me.

Hugo's the best little brother in the world but sometimes I get mad at him when he tries to eat my chocolate.

When he was born last year my nonna came to look after me. I was so happy when he was born that I took my mum in a bunch of yellow flowers.

That's Hugo on the left when he was six weeks old. Hasn't he grown up?

And this is me on the right. I've grown up too.

Guess what?

My mum is pregnant again so we will be getting a new baby very soon. We don't know if it will be a girl or a boy. What do you think? I love being a big brother and I will be so excited about this baby if it is a girl — or a boy.

As long as they don't try to eat my chocolate.

Contents

Why do you have to eat?

Feeling hungry? That's your body's way of telling you that it needs something to eat. Food has lots of goodness in it, which your body uses to grow, stay healthy and mend worn-out parts. Your food also gives you **energy**. Your body needs energy to make it go, just like a car needs petrol. You feel hungry when your energy supplies are running low.

AMAZING!

You eat an amazing 30 tonnes of food in your life – that's the weight of six elephants!

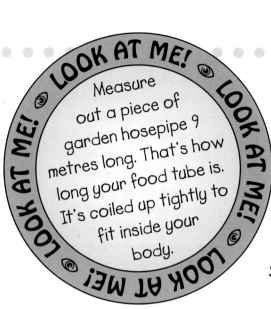

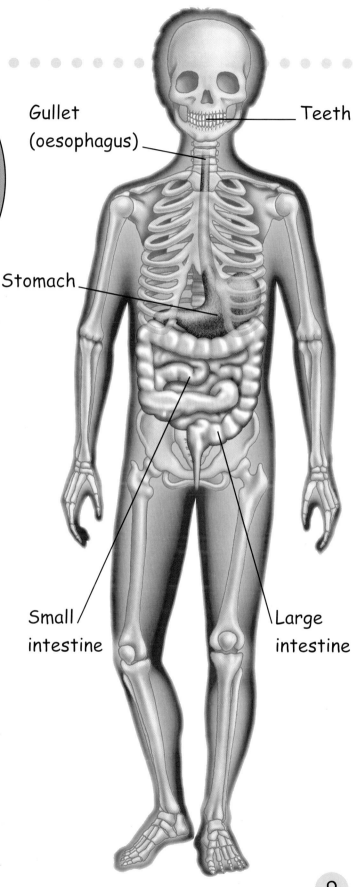

Gullet (oesophagus)

Teeth

Stomach

Small intestine

Large intestine

You eat a piece of yummy pizza. But where does your food go? Before your body can use the food, it has to break it into tiny bits. The bits have to be small enough to soak into your blood. Then your blood carries them around your body to all the parts that need them. This process is called **digestion**.

Your food is digested as it travels through your body. It travels through lots of different tubes, which go from your mouth to your bottom. You can see the different tubes in the picture on the right.

Chopping and chewing

Your body starts digesting your food as soon as you take your first bite. In your mouth, your teeth chop and chew the food into small pieces. Your tongue mashes the food up and pushes it to the back of your mouth. Your mouth also makes watery spit, called **saliva**. It wets the bits of food and makes them slippery and easy to swallow. That's why a delicious meal makes your mouth water.

AMAZING!

The outside of your teeth is made of strong **enamel**. It is the hardest part of your body.

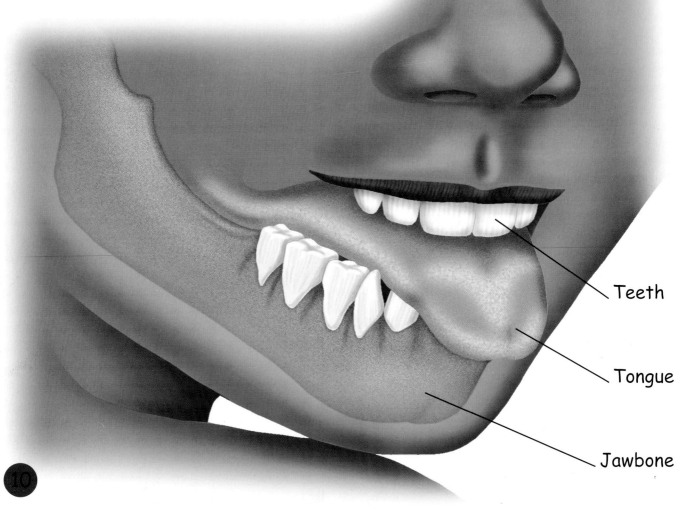

Teeth

Tongue

Jawbone

Run your tongue over your teeth. Can you feel that they are different shapes? Your front teeth are sharp for biting. Your back teeth are flat for crushing and grinding. When you are small, you have 20 little teeth, called milk teeth. These start to fall out when you are five or six years old, and 32 new, bigger teeth grow in their place.

LOOK AT ME! LOOK AT ME! LOOK AT ME! LOOK AT ME! LOOK AT ME!

Tiny bits of food stick to your teeth when you eat. You need to brush your teeth twice a day to get rid of them. Otherwise, your teeth can go bad.

How does it taste?

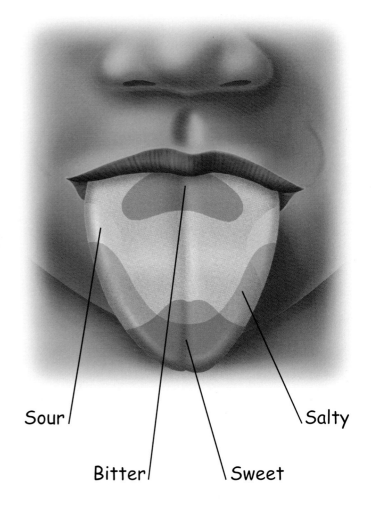

A slice of pizza tastes delicious. You taste it with your tongue. Look in a mirror and stick out your tongue. It is covered in thousands of tiny bumps, called **tastebuds**. They send messages along **nerves** to your brain to tell you what your food tastes like. Different parts of your tongue taste sweet, sour, salty and bitter things. Tasting is very useful. It tells you if food is good or bad to eat.

Sour

Salty

Bitter

Sweet

Your tastebuds as seen under a microscope.

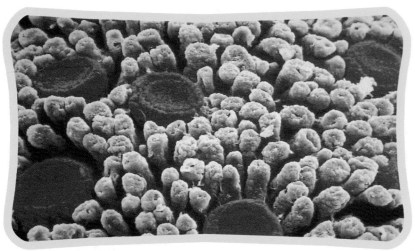

AMAZING!

You have more than 10,000 taste buds on your tongue but some of them stop working as you get older.

Tasty food often smells good, too. Your sense of smell helps you to pick up delicate flavours in your food. If you've got a cold and your nose is blocked up, you probably can't taste your food at all. This is because your senses of taste and smell are closely linked.

LOOK AT ME! LOOK AT ME! LOOK AT ME! LOOK AT ME!

When you eat a food with a strong taste, the next thing you eat tastes stronger. So, if you eat a sugary sweet, then a lemon, the lemon tastes bitter.

13

Swallowing

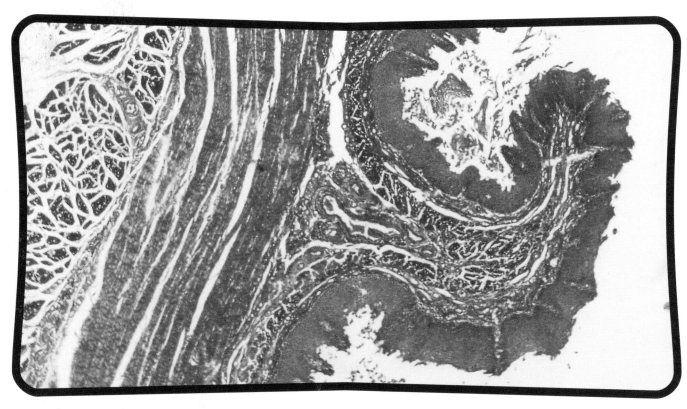

Muscles in the wall of your gullet, seen under a microscope.

After you've chewed your pizza, your tongue pushes it to the back of your mouth. Then you swallow it. The pizza goes into the first part of your food tube, which is called your gullet. But it does not slip or slide down. It is pushed along by strong muscles in the sides of your gullet. They squeeze to push the pizza along. This means that you could still eat and drink even if you were standing on your head!

AMAZING!

In one day, you swallow about 3,000 times! Gulp!

Sometimes your food goes down the 'wrong way' and makes you choke. This is because your gullet is next to your windpipe in your throat. You use your windpipe for breathing. Usually, a tiny flap covers the top of your windpipe when you swallow. But food sometimes goes down it by mistake.

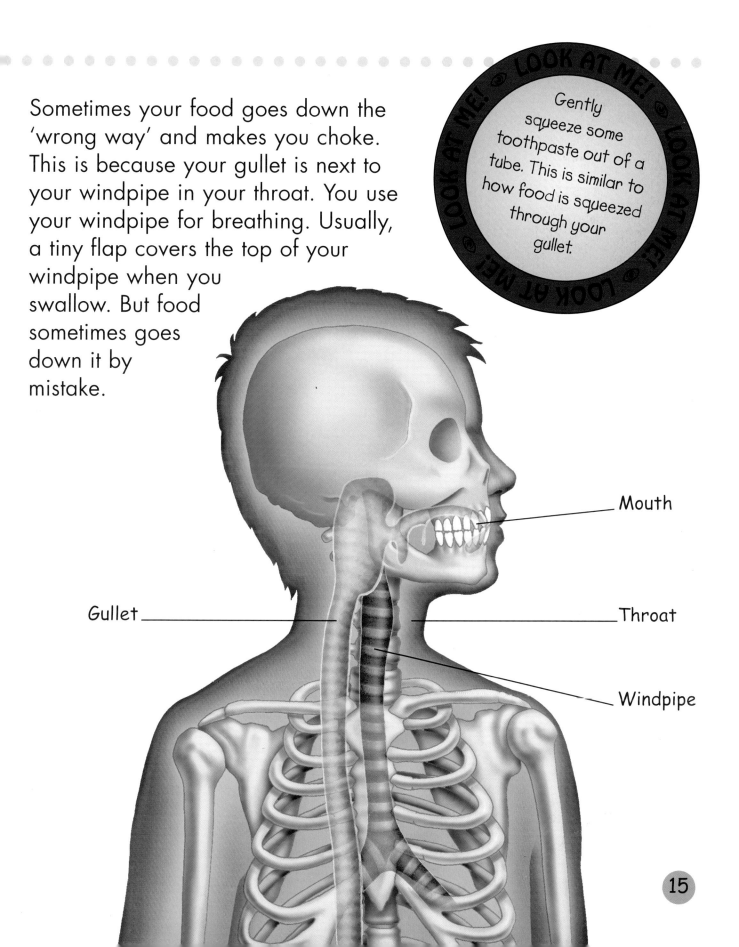

LOOK AT ME!

Gently squeeze some toothpaste out of a tube. This is similar to how food is squeezed through your gullet.

Mouth

Throat

Gullet

Windpipe

Inside your tummy

Your gullet squeezes your food into your stomach, or tummy. Your stomach is like a thick, stretchy bag made of strong muscle. It mashes and squashes the food up even more and pours special juices on to the food to break it up. The juices also help to kill any harmful **germs** in your food. Otherwise you might get tummy ache. By the time your food leaves your stomach, it looks like thick soup.

AMAZING!

A meal stays in your stomach for about four hours.
It takes about three days to travel right through you.

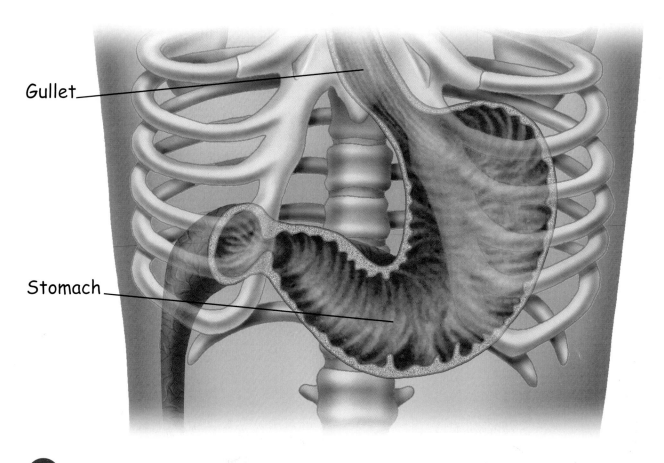

Gullet

Stomach

As your stomach fills up with food, it gets bigger. When it is full up, it sends messages to your brain to tell you not to eat any more. If you eat too much, or if you eat food that has gone bad, you might be sick. Then the muscles in your tummy force your food back up.

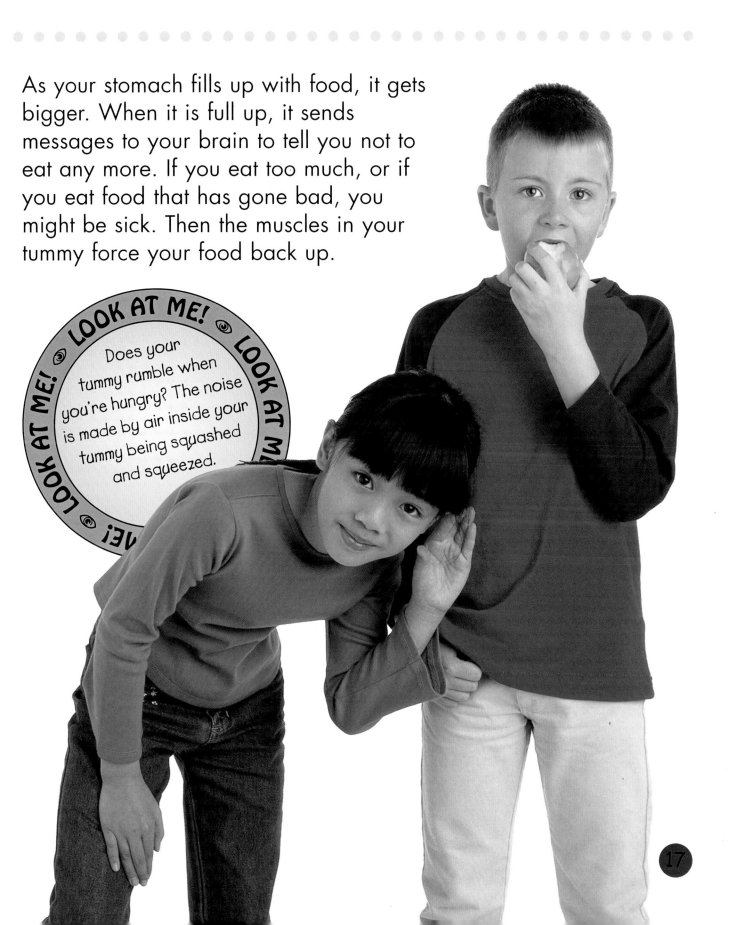

LOOK AT ME! LOOK AT ME! LOOK AT ME! LOOK AT ME!

Does your tummy rumble when you're hungry? The noise is made by air inside your tummy being squashed and squeezed.

A long journey

From your tummy, the thick soupy mixture is squeezed through a very long tube, called your small intestine. Your small intestine is as long as a bus but it is coiled up tightly inside you. More juices pour in to digest your food. By now the pieces are small enough to seep through the sides of your small intestine into your blood. Your blood carries them around your body to give you energy to grow and live.

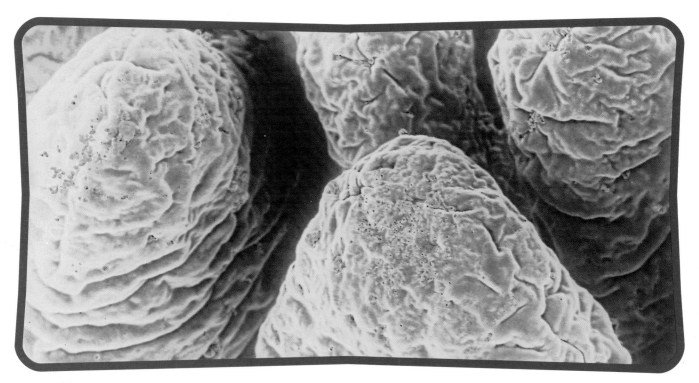

The walls of the small intestine, seen under a microscope. Your digested food seeps through the walls into your blood.

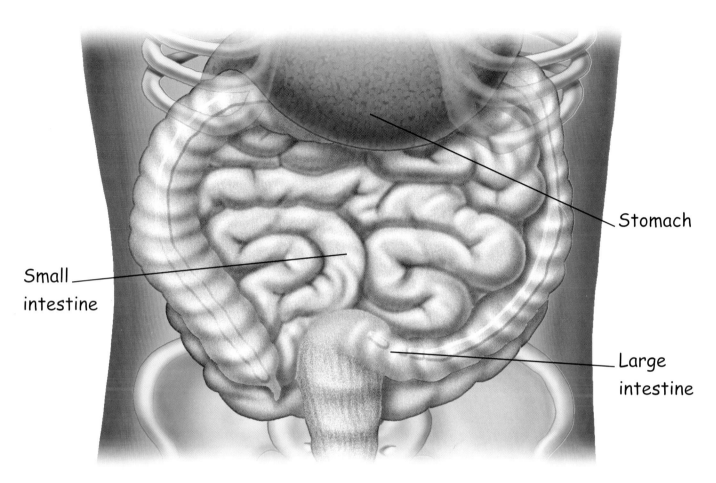

Stomach

Small intestine

Large intestine

LOOK AT ME! LOOK AT ME! LOOK AT ME! LOOK AT ME!

If you rush about after eating you might get **cramp** in your muscles. Your body is using its energy to digest your food and not to work your muscles!

Any parts of food that your body can't use are pushed into the next tube along. It is called your large intestine and is much shorter and wider than the small intestine. The waste food forms a soft, solid lump and is stored at the end of your large intestine. Then, when you go to the toilet, you push it out through a hole in your bottom.

Your liver and pancreas

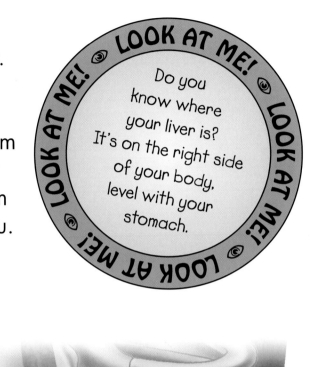

Your blood carries tiny bits of digested food all over your body. But first, it takes the food to your liver. Your liver does several important jobs. It takes some of the goodness from your food and stores it until your body needs it. It also cleans the poisons from your food so that they do not harm you. Then your blood takes the food to the rest of your body.

LOOK AT ME! LOOK AT ME! LOOK AT ME! LOOK AT ME!

Do you know where your liver is? It's on the right side of your body, level with your stomach.

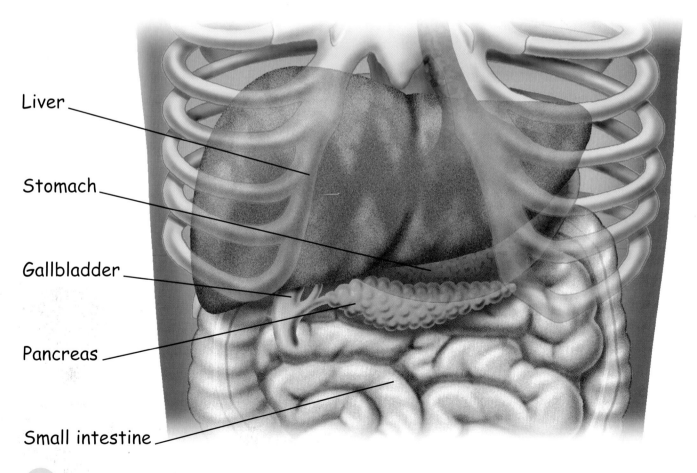

Liver

Stomach

Gallbladder

Pancreas

Small intestine

Your liver makes a green juice, called bile. It helps to break up the fatty bits in your food. The bile is stored in a small bag, called your gall bladder. Then it flows down a tiny tube into your small intestine. Your pancreas is another part of your body, which helps you to digest your food. It pours juices on to your food in your small intestine.

Some liver cells, as seen under a microscope.

AMAZING!

Your liver weighs about 1.5 kg. That's about the same as 10 apples.

Water works

Feeling thirsty? That's your body's way of telling you that it needs something to drink. Your body needs lots of water to make it work properly. But sometimes you take in more water than your body needs. You go to the toilet and get rid of the extra water in your **urine**.

LOOK AT ME! LOOK AT ME! LOOK AT ME! LOOK AT ME!

Urine is stored in your bladder. It can hold about as much liquid as two glasses of fizzy drink. But you'd be bursting for the toilet by then!

Urine is made in your kidneys. They work like tiny sieves. As your blood flows through your kidneys, they clean it and filter out any waste. They turn the waste into a yellow liquid, called urine. The urine trickles down two tubes into a small bag, called your bladder. It is stretchy, like a balloon. A tight muscle around your bladder stops urine from seeping out by accident. When you go to the toilet, the muscle loosens and lets the urine flow out along another tube.

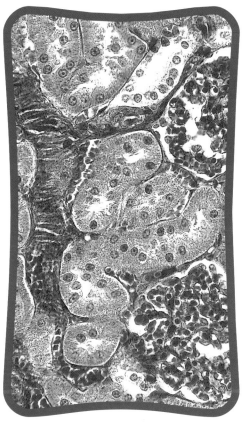

Tiny filters inside a kidney, seen under a microscope.

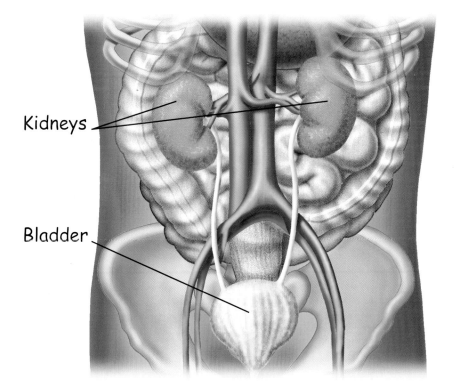

Kidneys

Bladder

AMAZING!

In your lifetime, you make enough urine to fill about 500 baths!

Healthy eating

Different kinds of food do different jobs in your body. You need to eat a good mixture of food to keep you healthy. This is called a balanced diet.

Foods, such as meat, fish and beans, make you grow and help repair worn-out bits of your body. Bread, rice, pasta and potatoes are good for giving you energy. Fruit and vegetables are full of goodness. They have **vitamins** and **minerals** in them that keep your body healthy and stop you getting ill. Milk, cheese and yoghurt make your bones and teeth strong.

LOOK AT ME!

Which of these meals do you think is best for you – sausage and chips or chicken, vegetables and rice?

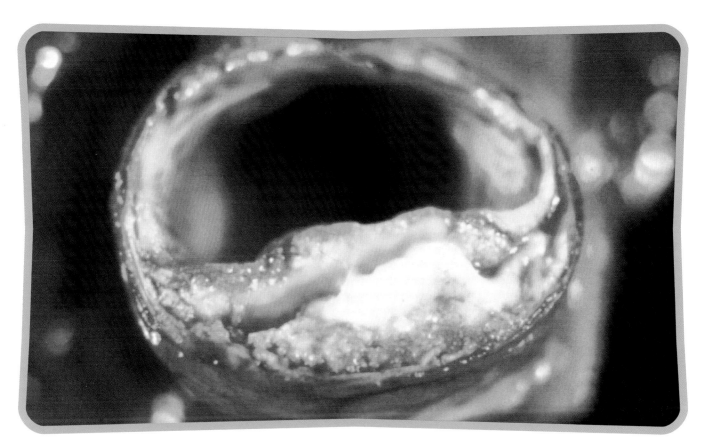

A blood vessel blocked with fat.

You also need to eat food that has fibre in it, such as brown bread. Fibre helps food to move through your body.

Fatty foods, such as cheese, sausages and sweet foods are also good for you. They give you energy and help to keep your blood healthy. But eating too much fat is bad for you. It blocks your blood vessels and stops blood getting to your heart.

AMAZING!

Some people think carrots help you to see in the dark. That's because they contain Vitamin A, which is good for your eyes.

Using up energy

The different kinds of food you eat give you different amounts of energy. Sweet foods and fatty foods have lots of energy in them. Salad has very little energy in it. The amount of energy in food is measured in **calories**. An apple has about 50 calories. A plate of pasta has about 250 calories. The food you buy from the supermarket has labels telling you how many calories it has in it.

AMAZING!

You could run about 1,000 metres on the amount of energy in a piece of pizza. But you could only run for 50 metres on a lettuce leaf.

Do you like swimming? You burn off 600 calories an hour when you swim. So why not dive in?

You use up lots of calories when you run, ride your bike or go swimming. Exercise is good for you because it keeps you fit and strong. Even sleeping uses up calories – about 70 calories an hour. If you eat too many calories and don't do enough exercise, it can make you overweight, which is bad for your health.

Glossary

Blood vessels The thin tubes which carry blood around your body.

Calories The units used to measure the amount of energy in your food.

Cramp A sharp pain you feel when a muscle suddenly squeezes very tight.

Digestion The way in which your body breaks down your food into such tiny pieces that it can pass into your blood.

Enamel An extra-hard substance which makes the tough outsides of your teeth.

Energy Your body needs energy to make it work and move. You get energy from the food you eat.

Germs Tiny living things which cause some illnesses.

Microscope An instrument used to look at objects which are too tiny to see otherwise.

Minerals Important substances in your food which your body needs to stay strong and healthy.

Nerves Special cells which carry messages between your body and your brain. They look like long wires.

Saliva A liquid made in your mouth. It helps you to swallow and makes your food easier to digest. It is also called spit.

Taste buds Tiny bumps on your tongue, which pick up different flavours in your food.

Urine The liquid you pass when you go to the toilet.

Vitamins Important substances in your food which your body needs to stay strong and healthy.

Index